0 8

Plea
dat
c

HOW does Science Work?

Materials

written by

Carol Ballard

WAYLAND

First published in Great Britain in 2007 by Wayland
An imprint of Hachette Children's Books

Copyright © 2007 Wayland

Hachette Children's Books
338 Euston Road, London NW1 3BH

Commissioning Editor: Vicky Brooker
Editors: Laura Milne, Camilla Lloyd
Senior Design Manager: Rosamund Saunders
Design and artwork: Peta Phipps
Commissioned Photography: Philip Wilkins
Consultant: Dr Peter Burrows
Series Consultant: Sally Hewitt

Printed and bound in China

Ballard, Carol
    Materials. - (How does science work?)
    1.Materials - Juvenile literature
    I.Title
    620.1'1

ISBN-10 0-7502-4799-1
ISBN-13 978-0-7502-4799-3

The website addresses (URLs) included in this book were valid at the time of going to press. However, because of the nature of the Internet, it is possible that some addresses may have changed, or sites may have changed or closed down since publication. While the authors and publishers regret any inconvenience this may cause the readers, no responsibility for any such changes can be accepted by either the author or the publisher.

Acknowledgements:

Cover photograph: A group of coloured balloons, Garry Gay/Alamy

Photo credits: Dana Neely/Getty Images 4, Raymond Gehman/Corbis 6, Joanna McCarthy/Getty Images 8, Darrin Jenkins/Alamy 10, Garry Gay/Alamy 11, David Hiser/Getty Images 12, Jean-Philippe Soule/Alamy 13, PicturePress/Getty Images 15, Janine Wiedel/Alamy 19, Marc Schlossman/Getty Images 22, Michael Paul/Corbis 23, Roy Morsch/Corbis 24, gkphotography/Alamy 25, John Humble/Getty Images 28.

The author and publisher would like to thank the models Kodie Briggs, Dylan Chen, Isabelle Li Murphy and Jessica Li Murphy.

Contents

Words in **bold** can be found in the glossary on p.30

Materials

We use materials to make things. You might be sitting on a wooden chair or reading a book made from paper. Wood and paper are both types of materials.

The clothes you are wearing are all made from materials, such as cotton for t-shirts, wool for jumpers and leather for shoes.

Buildings are made from many different materials too.

Many houses have walls made from brick or stone. Some, like this house, have walls made from wood.

TRY THIS! Find different materials

1. Look around the room that you are in.

2. Write a list of ten different things that you can see.

3. Next to each one, write down what it is made from.

You should be able to find many different materials.

Materials come from different places. Some of them come from under the ground and some come from plants or animals. These are all **natural materials**. Other materials are made by people and are called **man-made materials**.

Materials from the ground

Many materials come from the ground. Some are found near the **surface** but others are very deep underground.

Metals and **gems** are often buried deep below the ground. Long tunnels called mines are dug to reach them. Metals are used to make things, such as knives, coins, cars and aeroplanes. Gems can be used to make jewellery.

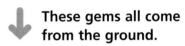
These gems all come from the ground.

TRY THIS! Make your own pot

1 You can make your own clay pot with modelling clay.

2 Roll out long sausages of clay.

3 Wind them round on top of each other. Bake the pot in the oven until it is hard.

You could paint your pot in different colours.

! Ask an adult to use the oven for you

Stone is often found nearer the surface of the ground. It is heavy and so it needs strong equipment to dig it out. Stone is used to make things, such as the walls of buildings and statues.

Clay is also found near the surface of the ground. It is easier than stone to dig out because it is softer. Plates, dishes, cups and vases can all be made from clay.

Rocks and soils

The surface of the Earth is made from rocks. Each type of rock has special **properties**. Rocks were formed millions of years ago. Different rocks were formed in different ways. Some rocks, such as chalk, were made from tiny sea creatures. When the creatures piled up at the bottom of seas and lakes, they were crushed and squashed together to make rocks.

Other rocks, such as granite, were formed deep inside the Earth. It is so hot below the surface of the Earth that the rocks are **liquid**. They cool and become **solid** as they rise to the surface.

When a volcano erupts, hot liquid rock shoots into the air. The air then cools it down and it becomes solid rock.

TRY THIS! Take a look at soil

1   You will need some soil from outside, a gardening sieve and a bucket to use as a container or a flat surface that you can get dirty.

2   Put some soil into a gardening sieve and shake it gently into the container.

3   Some of the soil should go through the sieve into the container but other twigs and stones might be left in the sieve.

You can see that there are lots of different things in the soil.

! **Wash your hands after touching soil**

Wind, rain, frost, ice and waves all damage rocks and tiny **fragments** break off. Soil contains these tiny pieces of rock. It also contains dead plants and animals, animal droppings and tiny creatures, such as worms and beetles.

Materials from plants

Plants provide us with many useful materials. Wood comes from the trunks and branches of trees. It is used to build houses and for parts of buildings, such as beams, floorboards and doors.

Cotton grows on cotton plants. It is picked and taken to factories where it is spun into long threads. These are woven together to make fabric for things, such as t-shirts, towels and sheets.

Wood is also used to make furniture like chairs and tables.

Rubber comes from a sticky juice, called **sap**. Sap can be found inside the trunks of rubber trees. A cut is made in the trunk and the sap trickles into a cup strapped to the trunk.

The stems and branches of plants, such as willow can be dried and woven together to make baskets and furniture.

Rubber can be used to make balloons, balls, elastic and car tyres.

The soles of many trainers, shoes and boots are made from rubber!

Materials from animals

Animals provide us with many useful materials. Wool comes from a sheep's coat. The wool is cut and then spun into threads. Wool is soft and warm and can be used to make things, such as jumpers and scarves, blankets and rugs.

Leather comes from the skins of animals. It is used to make shoes and bags.

In the Arctic, some people wear clothes made from animal fur to keep them warm. ➡

Feathers from birds such as ducks and geese are light and soft. They can be used as fillings for pillows, cushions and duvets. Brightly coloured feathers can also be used for decorations.

Silkworms spin **cocoons** of fine silk threads. The threads are woven into fabric.

Silk threads can be spun and woven into fabric to make beautiful clothes, such as these kimonos.

Man-made materials

Some materials are made by people. The material that you start with is called the **raw material**. The new material that is made is called a man-made material.

Plastic is a man-made material. The most important raw material used for making plastic is **oil**. The oil can be separated into different things. Some of these can be used to make plastic.

Wood is the raw material used to make paper. We can use paper for writing, to make books and for tissues.

Bottles, buckets and many of the things we use every day are made from plastic. →

Very high temperatures are needed to make this big glass container.

The raw materials needed to make glass are sand and limestone. These are mixed together and heated. When the mixture gets very, very hot, it turns into glass. Windows, light bulbs and drinking glasses are made from glass.

Looking at properties

We can explain what a material is like
by talking about its properties.
Think about how you would describe a
material such as wood. Is it hard or soft?
Is it strong or weak? Is it rough or smooth?
Is it **absorbent** or **waterproof**?

These are just some of the
different properties a
material may have.

**Bricks are hard
but cotton
wool is soft.** →

TRY THIS! Test a material's properties

1 You will need to collect some small objects made from different materials like wool, some coins and a pebble.

2 List them down one side of a piece of paper.

3 Draw lines to make four more columns down the page.

4 Choose four properties to test the materials for and write them as headings for the columns.

5 Test the first object for each property in turn. You could touch the object to test whether it is hard or soft. Try pulling it to see if it is elastic. Hold it next to a magnet to test whether or not it is magnetic. After each test, put a ✔ or a ✘ in your table.

6 Then test the rest of the objects for each property until all the boxes are complete.

7 Do any of your materials have exactly the same set of properties?

You can use your chart to help describe each material. For example, an elastic band is soft and elastic.

	hard	soft	elastic	magnetic
wool	✘	✔	✘	✘
elastic band	✘	✔	✔	✘
metal coin				
paper				
pebble				
cushion				

Using materials

It is important to choose materials with the right properties for how they will be used. Can you imagine chairs made from jelly and an umbrella made from a towel?

Materials have different properties. This means that some are better for one job than others. An umbrella is meant to stop rain getting through, so it needs to be made with a waterproof material.

A cushion is meant to be comfortable to sit on, so a soft material is used.

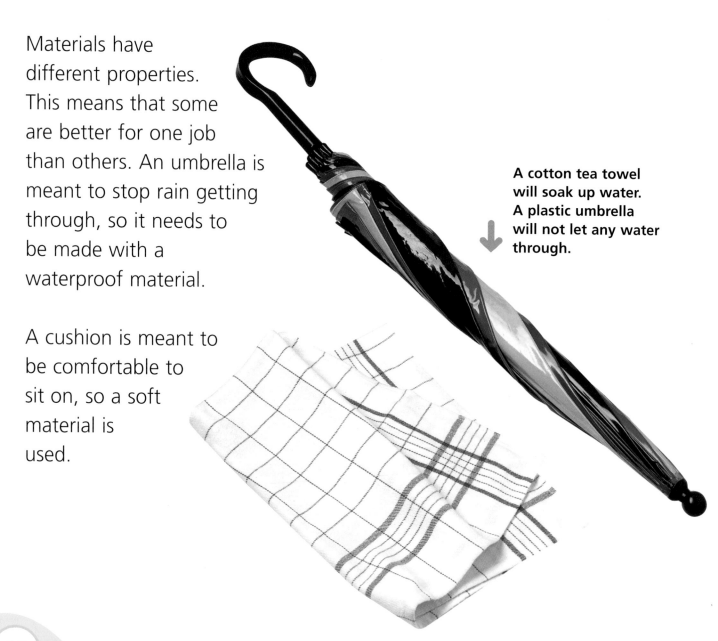

A cotton tea towel will soak up water. A plastic umbrella will not let any water through.

If you look around your bedroom at home or your school classroom you will see that lots of different materials have been used. Tables and chairs need to be made from something strong and **rigid** so they are often made from wood, metal or plastic.

Are your classroom desks made of wood like these?

Materials for warmth

Materials that do not let heat travel through them are called **thermal insulators**. Wood, wool and fleecy fabrics are all good thermal insulators and keep in warmth.

Warm clothes in winter can help to trap our body heat and keep the cold air out.

Thermal insulators can also keep heat out. Packing a chilled picnic in a thermal picnic bag helps to keep it cool because it does not let the warm air in.

To keep our bodies warm in cold weather, we can put on hats, scarves, gloves and jumpers made from wool or fleecy materials.

TRY THIS! Find thermal insulators

1. You will need to collect a thermometer and some similar-sized containers made of different materials, such as a metal can, a mug and a glass.

2. Ask an adult to help you heat some water.

3. Pour the same amount of water into each container.

4. Use a thermometer to measure the temperature of the water.

5. After five minutes, measure the temperature of the water in each container.

6. Repeat after ten and fifteen minutes.

You should find that the water stays hotter in some containers than in others. This is because some materials are better thermal insulators than others.

Take care with hot water

Materials that let heat travel through them are called **thermal conductors**. Metals and glass are good thermal conductors. Radiators and irons are made of metals, to allow heat to travel through them easily.

Solids and liquids

Some materials change from a liquid to a solid and back again when they are heated or cooled down.

When water is very cold it turns to solid ice. As it warms up, it **melts** and becomes a liquid.
If you put it back in the freezer, it cools. When it gets cold enough, it **freezes** and becomes a solid again.

Ice cream melts quickly on a hot day but it will turn back to a solid if it is frozen. Remember it is not good to eat ice cream if it has been frozen twice.

When runny chocolate cools down, it slowly becomes hard and solid again.

Other materials change as they get hotter or colder too. For example, butter will melt and become soft and runny on a hot day but if you put it back in the fridge it will become hard and solid again.

Wow!

At very high temperatures, even metals and rocks can turn into runny liquids!

Water and steam

What happens to water when it heats up? When water gets hot enough, it **boils** and turns into a **gas** that we call **steam**. The steam disappears into the air.

It is harder to see, but the same thing is happening when a puddle dries up. The water turns into steam and becomes part of the air.

The water in this pan is boiling and is turning into steam.

When steam cools down again, it turns back into liquid water. You can see this happen in a steamy bathroom when water droplets form on cold surfaces such as mirrors and windows.

If you breathe out on a cold day your breath looks white in the air. This is because the steam in your breath turns back to liquid water when it meets the cold air outside.

Horses' breath turns white when it meets the cold air.

Changed forever

Burning, cooking, and **rusting** all change materials forever. Adding heat to materials makes them change. If we add enough heat, many materials will burn. Once a material has burned, you cannot change it back. It turns into soot and ashes, and gases are released into the air. This is what happens when you burn materials like paper or wood.

When you make toast, you cannot change it back into fresh bread again.

TRY THIS! Change a material forever

1 Squeeze some juice from a lemon into a bowl.

2 Add a teaspoon of baking powder and stir gently.

3 Watch what happens.

The mixture should froth and make bubbles. You cannot get back the lemon juice and baking powder that you started with.

Cooking changes materials forever. For example, when you bake a cake in a hot oven, the heat changes the runny mixture into a solid cake. You cannot get the runny cake mixture back again.

Recycling materials

Our raw materials will not last forever. So we should try to **recycle** materials.

Recycling means to use things again. A lot of what we throw away can be recycled. This saves raw materials and also means we have less waste.

Glass bottles, jars and other containers can be heated until they melt. The liquid glass can then be used to make new bottles. Metals can be recycled in the same way.

Wow!

Did you know that many fleecy jackets are made from recycled plastic bottles?

↑ **Plastic bottles and bags can be recycled.**

TRY THIS! Make your own paper

1 You will need a wooden frame, like an old, unused picture frame, some thin fabric, newspaper and a bowl of water.

2 Stretch the fabric over the frame and staple it in place.

3 Tear the old newspaper into small pieces and soak them in a bucket of water overnight.

4 Pour off most of the water and squeeze the rest together to make a sticky pulp.

5 Spread this evenly over the fabric and gently press it flat. Cover it with a cloth and leave it to dry.

! Ask an adult to use the stapler for you

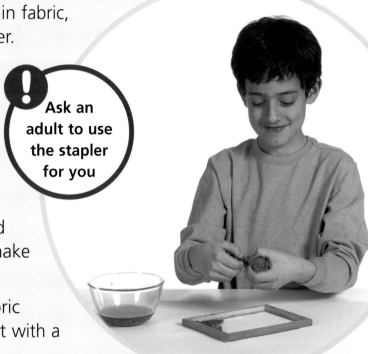

When you go back to the dry pulp you should be able to peel your own recycled piece of paper off the fabric.

Cardboard and paper can be mixed with water to make a paste. This can then be used to make new cardboard and paper. Recycling paper means we cut down fewer trees.

Glossary

absorbent soaks up liquids

boils when a liquid turns into a gas - for example, liquid water to steam

coccoons silky cases where caterpillars change into adult butterflies or moths

fragments the broken off parts of something

freezes when a liquid becomes so cold that it turns into a solid – for example, liquid water to solid ice

gas a gas has no shape and can be invisible, air is a mixture of gases

gems stones that come from under the ground

liquid a runny material that takes the shape of its container

man-made materials materials made by people

melts when a solid is heated to become a liquid – for example, solid ice to liquid water

metals hard materials found under the ground

natural materials materials that come from animals, plants or the Earth

oil a greasy liquid that is found under rocks beneath the Earth's surface

properties what materials are like

raw material a natural material which is used to make a new material

recycle to use again

rigid stiff, not bendy

rusting the slow change from shiny iron to reddish-brown rust

sap juice inside a plant stem

solid a material that keeps its own shape

steam the gas that is made when water is heated

surface the topmost layer of something

thermal conductors materials that heat can travel through

thermal insulators materials that heat cannot travel through

waterproof does not let in water

Further information

Books to read

Changing Materials by Robert Sneddon, Materials All Around Us series, Heinemann Library, 2002

Materials by Claire Llewellyn, Evans Brothers, 2004

How Do We Use Materials? by Jacqui Bailey, Franklin Watts Ltd, 2002

How We Use...series by Chris Oxlade, Carol Ballard *et al*, Raintree Perspectives: Using Materials, Raintree, 2005

Solids, Liquids and Gases: From Ice Cubes to Bubbles by Carol Ballard, Science Answers series, Heinemann Library, 2003

Websites to visit

www.bbc.co.uk/education/ dynamo

Full of experiments you can do at home.

www.bbc.co.uk/schools/ scienceclips

Lots of interesting information and quizzes to test your knowledge.

CD Roms to explore

Play and Learn: Science Experiments, Dorling Kindersley, 2000

Become a Science Explorer, Dorling Kindersley, 2000

Index